# WATCH THEM
# GROW

## Written by Linda Martin

DORLING KINDERSLEY
LONDON • NEW YORK • STUTTGART

A DORLING KINDERSLEY BOOK

**Written and edited by** Linda Martin
**Designer** Ingrid Mason
**Editorial Consultant** Theresa Greenaway
**Illustrators** Sandra Pond, Will Giles
**Production** Catherine Semark
**Deputy Editorial Director** Sophie Mitchell
**Deputy Art Director** Miranda Kennedy

First published in Great Britain in 1994 by Dorling Kindersley Limited,
9 Henrietta Street, London, WC2E 8PS

Reprinted 1997
Copyright © 1994 Dorling Kindersley Limited, London
Visit us on the World Wide Web at
http://www.dk.com

A CIP catalogue record for this book is available from the British Library

ISBN 0-7513-5135-0

Colour reproduction by Colourscan, Singapore
Printed and bound in Italy by L.E.G.O.

# Contents

# All sorts of babies

Many baby animals and plants change as they grow. What do you think these babies will look like when they are grown up?

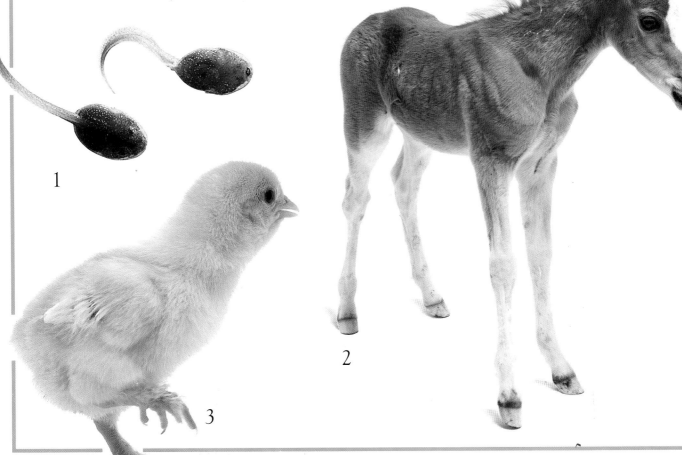

1

2

3

The answers are on page 45

5

4

6

7

8

9

10

9

# Being born

Can you guess what these baby
animals will grow into? See if
you can match them up
with their mothers
on the next page.

1

2

3

4

Each one of
these baby
animals feeds on
its mother's milk.
They are all
mammals.

5

6

Sheep

Dog

Tiger

Wolf

All these
grown-up
animals
are furry.

Kangaroo

Rabbit

The answers are on page 45

# Cat

A baby cat is called a kitten. A kitten looks rather scruffy when it is born. But watch this one grow into a sleek, silky cat like her mother.

## 1 Just born

A newborn kitten is very sleepy.

A newborn kitten is covered with fur. It cannot see or hear.

## 2 Eyes open

Two weeks later, the kitten can see and hear. She moves around too.

# 3 Full of fun

The kitten becomes more and more lively as she grows stronger. She spends a lot of her time playing.

A ball of wool is one of the kitten's favourite toys.

# 4 Quite grown up

The kitten eats the same food as her parents now.

At ten weeks old, the kitten is a young cat. She has grown a lot, hasn't she? But she needs to grow even more before she can have kittens of her own.

# Rabbit

A baby rabbit is very odd! It is bald, wrinkly, and not at all pretty! It is not a bit like a cuddly grown-up rabbit.

## 1 Just born

A newborn rabbit has no fur. Its eyes are shut and it cannot hear. It is very sleepy.

## 2 Soft fur

Soft fur has started to grow. But the rabbit's eyes are still shut and he cannot hear yet.

# 3  Looking for adventure

Now that the rabbit can see and hear, he starts to explore. He doesn't wander too far away though.

This grass looks good enough to eat!

Eating lots of lettuce will help him grow big and strong.

# 4  Long ears

The young rabbit is six weeks old and is much bigger. Look how his ears have grown! He is very cuddly now, isn't he?

# Dog

A baby dog is called a puppy. A puppy grows quite slowly. It takes more than a year for the puppy to grow as big as its mother.

## 1 Just born

A newborn puppy cannot see or hear.

A puppy is born with lots of fur. It only wakes up when it is hungry!

## 2 Eyes open

A puppy's nose is very short!

The puppy walks about as soon as he can see where he is going!

## 3 Playful pup

As the puppy grows, he spends more and more time playing. His fur is thick and fluffy now.

## 4 A young dog

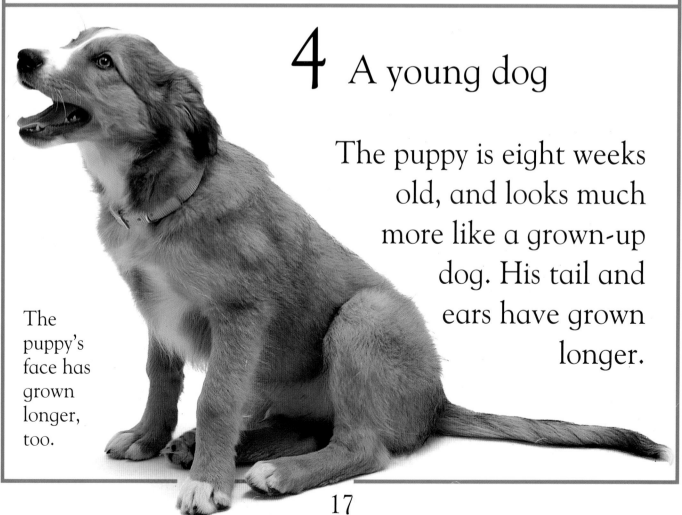

The puppy's face has grown longer, too.

The puppy is eight weeks old, and looks much more like a grown-up dog. His tail and ears have grown longer.

# Horse

A baby horse is called a foal. A foal looks like its mother when it is born, but it is much smaller.

## 1 Long legs

A foal runs about on its long legs soon after being born.

A foal can see and hear when it is born.

## 2 Growing up

The foal grows bigger and stronger every day.

# 3 Munching apples

The growing foal gallops around the fields every day. This makes him very hungry. He eats apples as well as grass now.

# 4 Long tail

The foal's body and legs are fatter, too.

The foal is five months old. His coat is shiny brown and his tail and mane are beginning to grow longer. It will be at least another year before he is as big as his mother though.

# Eggs

Some baby animals hatch from eggs. Do you think you can guess what will hatch from these eggs? Look for their mothers on the next page.

1

2

3

4

5

6

Spider

Owl

Duck

Dogfish

Snake

Lizard

The answers are on page 45

21

# Chicken

Watch this fluffy chick grow up to look like its father. It will look quite different from its mother.

## 1 Hatching

A chick is hatching from an egg laid by its mother. It is very wet, isn't it?

## 2 Soft and fluffy

The chick's feathers are soft and fluffy now. He loves to eat seeds.

# 3 Changing colour

This chick is growing bigger. His fluffy yellow feathers have fallen out and new grey ones have grown instead.

This chick still does not look like its father, does he?

# 4 Red head

Now this chick is eight weeks old. Most of his adult feathers have grown and he has a red "comb" on his head, just like his father.

The chick's long, black tail feathers have not grown yet.

23

# Duck

Ducklings grow very quickly. It takes only a few weeks for this duckling to grow into a fine white duck like her mother.

## 1 Hatching

The duckling pushes its way out of the egg laid by its mother.

## 2 Splash!

After only two days, the duckling goes for her first swim. She loves it!

# 3 New feathers

The duckling is changing shape. She is not as round as she was before. Her baby feathers are falling out. New white feathers are growing in their place.

# 4 Fine wings

The duckling's short yellow beak has grown into a long orange one.

The duckling is six weeks old. All her feathers are white and her wings are big and strong. Soon she will fly for the first time.

 # Parrot

Look at this funny chick! Will he really grow into a green parrot like his father? His mother is red and blue.

## 1 Just hatched

A parrot has no feathers at all when it hatches.

## 2 Fluffy fellow

Feathers are growing now. But they are grey!

# 3 Going green!

The green feathers show that this chick is male.

The parrot chick is four weeks old. Green feathers are beginning to grow now.

The young parrot's long tail feathers still have to grow.

# 4 Nearly grown up

The young parrot is eight weeks old. He has lost all his fluffy grey feathers. Isn't it amazing that this fine fellow could grow from that funny, bald chick?

27

# Frog

Some creatures that hatch out of eggs look nothing like their parents! See how a tadpole grows into a frog.

## 1 Hatching

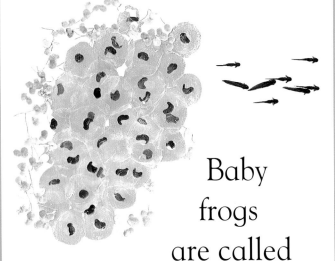

Baby frogs are called tadpoles. They hatch from eggs laid in water.

## 2 Eating

Tadpoles eat all the time. They grow fatter and rounder every day.

# 3 Growing legs

Tiny legs begin to grow. The back legs grow first, then the front legs.

# 4 Vanishing tail

As the tadpole's legs grow longer, its tail gets shorter and shorter.

# 5 Little frog

The little frog slowly grows up to look like its parents. It uses its strong back legs to jump about.

The little frog is three months old. It has lost its tail, but still has to grow a lot.

# Fish

Some fish hatch from eggs. These baby fish are sticklebacks. They take two years to grow into adults like their mother and father.

## 1 Fish eggs

The brown mother fish lays lots of eggs like these in the water.

## 2 Tiny fish

The father fish looks after the tiny fish when they hatch.

# 3 Young fish

The young fish
soon grow bigger.
They eat small
shrimps, insects,
and sometimes
other fish!

# 4 Which colour?

If this fish is female,
it will turn a dull,
yellowy-brown like
its mother. Which
colour do you
think it will be?

This growing
fish is shiny brown. If it is male,
it will turn red, blue, and silver when
it is grown up — just like its father.

# Butterfly

A fat caterpillar looks very different from its mother! Watch how this one turns into a beautiful, fluttering butterfly.

## 1 Hatching

A caterpillar climbs out of an egg that its mother laid.

## 2 Growing

The caterpillar changes colour too.

The caterpillar eats and eats.

# 3 Changing

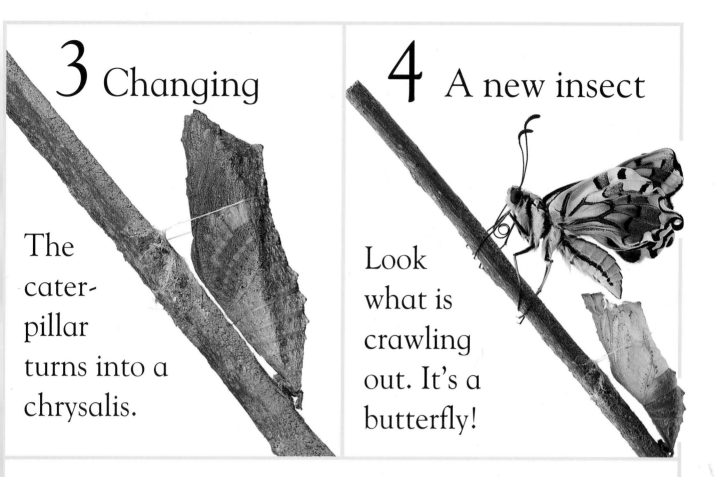

The cater-pillar turns into a chrysalis.

# 4 A new insect

Look what is crawling out. It's a butterfly!

# 5 Fine wings

In a hot summer, the new butterfly is ready to lay its own eggs just eight weeks after the caterpillar hatched.

# Seeds

Flowers grow from seeds. So do trees, fruits, and vegetables. Seeds are all sorts of sizes, shapes, and colours – like these. Did you know that all these are seeds?

1

2

3

What do you think these will grow into? Look at the next page for clues.

4

5

6

The answers are on
page 45

Pea pod

Chestnut

Strawberry

Lemon

Dandelion

Sunflower

35

# Bean

Do you like to eat green beans? Each bean is really a seed that could grow into a whole new bean plant. It won't grow inside your tummy though!

## 1 Splitting skin

The root grows down into the ground.

A seed begins to grow in the ground. First, its skin splits and a tiny root appears.

## 2 Shooting up

A shoot appears. This grows up towards the light.

Tiny rootlets grow from the main root.

# 3 Leaves

The shoot continues to grow upwards. After it has broken through the soil, leaves appear on the stem.

# 4 Flowers

The bean plant grows very fast. Small red flowers open. After the petals fall off, tiny pods form.

Young bean seeds grow inside the pods. When the pods burst, the seeds fall to the ground.

# Poppy

Have you ever seen a field full of poppies? Each poppy plant grows from a tiny black seed. But where does the seed come from?

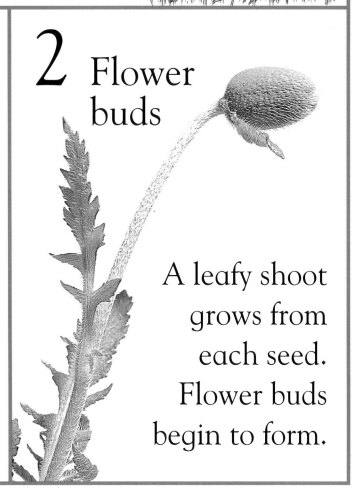

## 1 Poppy pods

Poppy seeds are shaken from poppy pods when the wind blows.

The seeds fall to the ground.

## 2 Flower buds

A leafy shoot grows from each seed. Flower buds begin to form.

# 3 Pretty flowers

Each bud is the beginning of a poppy flower. As a bud opens, a beautiful flower unfolds.

A poppy plant has lots of buds. But each flower only lasts for one day.

# 4 Falling petals

After the petals fall, seed heads, called pods, form.

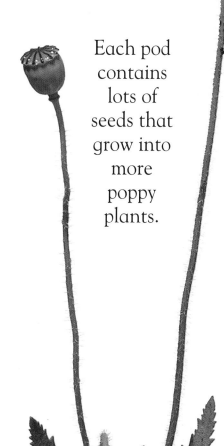

Each pod contains lots of seeds that grow into more poppy plants.

# Apple

Some very big things grow from tiny seeds. An apple tree like this takes several years to grow from a small seed.

## 1 Pips

The tiny pips that you see when you bite into an apple are seeds.

## 2 Blossom

Pretty flowers, called blossom, grow on an apple tree.

# 3 Tiny apples

After the blossom falls off, tiny green apples begin to grow on the branches of the tree.

Each branch of an apple tree may be covered with growing apples.

# 4 Juicy fruit

Some apples turn red, some turn yellow, and others stay green.

Each little apple slowly grows into a large apple. The tasty part you eat protects the seeds inside.

# Toadstool

A toadstool grows from a special kind of seed called a spore. Toadstools grow very quickly. This one grew in just one day!

## 1 Tiny buds

Tiny threads grow from spores underneath the ground. These threads grow into a small bud.

## 2 Pushing up

A bud pushes its way up out of the ground.

# 3 Growing up

As the stalk shoots up, the cap on top begins to open.

A toadstool cap opens out like an umbrella.

# 4 Fully grown

Spores are so tiny you can hardly see them.

The new toadstool has flaps, called gills, underneath its cap. These gills make spores that fall to the ground.

# Changes

Now you know that some babies look like their parents – apart from being smaller. Others are a different shape or colour, or both!

A baby ladybird is a different colour and shape.

A red pepper changes from green to red as it ripens.

A baby swan is grey, but its parents are sparkling white.

# Index

**Photographers:** Jane Burton, Gordon Clayton, Geoff Dann, Richard Davies, Phillip Dowell, Neil Fletcher, Frank Greenaway, Dave King, Andrew McRobb, Roger Phillips, Karl Shone, Kim Taylor, Jerry Young, Barrie Watts.

Additional design assistance: Sharon Grant, Mark Haygarth, Tina Robinson

**Answers from pages 8/9**: 1 = Frog; 2 = Horse; 3 = Cockerel; 4 = Parrot; 5 = Cuttlefish; 6 = Stickleback; 7 = Bean plant; 8 = Butterfly; 9 = Poppy plant; 10 = Cat.
**Answers from pages 10/11**: 1 = Tiger; 2 = Dog; 3 = Sheep; 4 = Rabbit; 5 = Wolf; 6 = Kangaroo.
**Answers from pages 20/21**: 1 = Spider; 2 = Duck; 3 = Dogfish; 4 = Lizard; 5 = Snake; 6 = Owl.
**Answers from pages 34/35**: 1 = Lemon; 2 = Pea; 3 = Sunflower; 4 = Dandelion; 5 = Strawberry; 6 = Chestnut.